# Letters from the Sister of Sorrows

Elysia Raine Henry

# contents

# The Sister of Sorrows

I am the lonely cry of the night's wind

I am the chill in an unshared bed

I am the tears wetting lips that have never been kissed

The trembling hand that has never been held

I am the void that nothing can fill, yet threatens to consume what holds it

And yet, I am a single rose blooming in the desert

For where there is pain, there is also beauty and strength


I am the Sister of Sorrows

Return to me, oh Sister of Sorrows

Let my heart beat once more to your banshee call

Cloak me in your unending night

Sail me up upon your wings through moonless sky bereft of starlight

Let us dance together in joyous mourning

You for I, and I for you

Let us find in each other that which the world has mocked us with

Before even I knew your name, you were there watching

Waiting for me to call to you and take your tender hand in mine

Come, and we shall sleep together, wrapped in each other's embrace

Until the world ends, and oblivion find us all


For we are the Sisters of Sorrow

Riding through the night on the tail of the wind
She raises her voice in lament once more
The Sister of Sorrows
Blessed Mother of the lonely
Comforter of the broken
Healer of the shattered
A double-edged sword is the melody that she sings
To those who hear her cry, it is the dulcet tones of hope and peace
A kindred soul
One who would take them in and mend their wounds
But to her
To our dear sweet Sister, they are the lacerations upon her heart
The tears shed in sadness
The aching of a lonely house
Sister of Sorrows?
Yes, that is her name now, but not who she once was
Born as the Maiden of Misfortune, her life's path called her to a new identity
Fueled by the cruelty of others, she became the Sister of Solitude
High in the sky did she build her castle, where none could reach her
She would often return to the ground, to see if the world outside had changed
It had, but only for the worse
When the pain became too great for her, she grasped on to it
Embraced it
Breathed it in to the depths of her soul
Like wine from a cup overflowing
She drank its essence and became one with it
The Sister of Sorrows
And when she had drank her fill, she took up her cloak and dagger
Screaming through the night that She was ready
She would be there
And she would steal that cup from as many as would let her
So that they would not have to know of its bitter, soul-sucking taste
She is the Sister of Sorrows
Mother to the Mournful

Long may she fight

In the dark night of the soul, she comes to me

The one who has never left my side since birth

My consort, the Sister of Sorrows

Placing a hand upon my shoulder, she leans over me

Her other wiping dry the tears that sit upon my cheek

She moves to sit beside me, long, dark hair blowing in the wind

Her head now on my shoulder, she wraps her cloak around me, giving protection

from the cold

She speaks no words, but instead just holds me

Providing warmth and comfort

The softness of her touch, the heat of her breath

They remind me that I am still here

That I will continue to be here

That she will never leave

Running fingers through my hair, she whispers

The words are inaudible, and yet I feel them in my heart

They do not bring strength

Nor do they heal the scars which run so deep

No, hope is the gift that they possess

It is but a tiny flicker, yet it is enough to keep the flame from winking out

Throughout the darkness of the night she sits

The chilling tendrils that can only come forth from the Void break against our backs

Licking against us, but unable to take hold

Until the first light of dawn breaks across the horizon

Lulled to sleep by her gentle touch, I rise

Finding only her cloak laid over me, a ring tied around my neck

A promise that she will always return

My Queen of Sorrows

Last night my lover came to visit

The Sister of Sorrows, who is never far from my heart

She took my head in her tender hands and held me as my world collapsed beneath me

Gently, she rocked me as I sobbed, holding me in her loving embrace

She whispered into my ears the words I needed to hear

That she would never leave me

That I would be strong again

Her voice, melodic and pure, soothed my soul and calmed my fears

When finally, I could cry no more, she wrapped her cloak around me

Placed her crown upon my head

And bade me rise up

Reborn through pain

To assume my place at her side

Her Queen of Sorrows.

Come and sit with me for a while Dearheart

Let me wrap you In my embrace

Give unto me those things that trouble you; your burdens and your fears

I will cast them into the great emptiness beyond

Give to me your deepest secrets, your wildest passions, and your strongest dreams

Your most fervent hopes

I will lock them away in my heart of hearts, where they cannot be disturbed by your foes

When you are saddened, let my cloak be a comfort to you

When you are overwhelmed, scream all your fury in to me

You will never erode my strength

When you cry, sit by my side and cry into me

You will never fill me up

I have been there for you since before the beginning, since before you knew my name

As I will be for all time, for in the end, you will come in wholeness to me

And we will dance for eternity in the most intimate of embraces

- A message from the Void to her beloved

Take the pieces of my broken heart

Gather them up and place them in a basket

Color some with sadness

Some with longing

And others with betrayal

Take the shards and fragments and arrange them in a lovely picture

Stained glass to hang in the Hall of Memories

Admire its beauty, the pain and labour that went into its creation

When you tire of it, smash it

Recolor it

Reshape it

Turn it into another testament of survival

Of conflict

Of loss

Repeat this process as many times as you desire

And when there is nothing left

When the pieces have been shattered into little more than dust

Let the wind carry them on its breath

And for a brief moment, see the sunlight glint off of them as though they were diamonds

I have danced with frivolity and felt the ecstasy of the stars' touch as they danced with me.

So too have I danced with Death, and gazed longingly into his eyes.

He was not strong enough to capture me.

I have known the pain of rejection, and I have grown stronger for it, each time building another step to help me upwards.

My faith in Love has never waned.

I have learned that pain is as a rose, if you clip it at its bud, you will never see its beauty.

I have, at great cost to myself, become the villain, crushing a dear one's dream before it progressed to places I could not travel.

I risk all that I know and am for me dream, but still I face it.

Is it better to live a lie, or to have never lived?

Both are the same.

I have flirted with joy, yet never for long, we are as ships on the wind.

To see her unfamiliar face would be a sight indeed.

Love is my purpose, the sole reason for my existence.

Not to tell a special one of my affection, but to show an unspecial one they have worth.

Although it is my greatest strength, so too is it my weakness, for there are those who would manipulate and use that.

Perhaps I should not be so cautious.

Though my soul be as water, susceptible to other influences, I will stand in the flames.

What fire can burn hotter than one with uninhibited passion.

At the end of all things, I have stood high upon the mountain, low upon the beach, and with voice lifted heavenward said, "Yes, I will go!"

Though it be as a whisper to some, barely audible to most, to the universe it was a mighty shout.

For I am still here.

I am broken.

Like the jagged pieces of a shattered window, if handled carelessly, I will hurt you.

However,

A gentle hand,

A tender touch,

Time spent carefully arranging the fragments of my heart…

These things will restore me to more than the sum of my parts.

I am broken,

But do not think for one moment that I have no value.

It is in my brokenness that I find my worth.

Like a piece of clay that the potter is not satisfied with, I can be remolded.

This will take dedication, a love of creating, and time.

Works of art are not produced quickly, and there is much pain that goes into them.

Yet, if you do not lose hope, I will be your masterpiece.

Your one-of-a-kind creation.

I am a stained-glass window, ornately crafted, fitting for the most grandiose of cathedrals.

Some assembly required.

I am the Hedgehog.

I will hurt you.

It is not something done intentionally, but reactionary.

If you persist through the stings and jabs, you will find someone to comfort you,

Someone to be by your side,

Someone who is yours and yours alone.

But it will take time,

And love, both yours and mine,

For I am broken.

Rapunzel, Rapunzel

See her sitting in a tower so high

High

High

Closed off from the world

Her tower of steel and stone

(Protection)


"Who put you there?"

Ask the gallant knights

Approaching on snow white horses

Silken hair

Gleaming teeth

Come to save her

(They can't)


But try they must

For she is a princess to be saved

So they climb up

Up

Up

High above the clouds

(Foolish determination)


And when they slip

(They always do)

She wipes a tear

As she journeys down to where they fell

To collect their dented armour

And build her tower higher

(A monster in her den)

Will I ever stop loving her?

Don't be foolish, my child.

You know that all things must end.

When?

Not too far off, by my measure.

After her sight has long since faded from these eyes.

After the breath of life no longer courses through these lungs.

When the sun has swelled and scorched the Earth.

When the last star in the last galaxy has blinked out.

Then my love for her may have lessened.

For all eternity is but a moment with her.

And a moment without her, an eternity.

When will I stop loving her?

Easy, my child.

When the end of all days has come,

And we are all as one with the Creator.

It is only but a moment away.

I have seen your face in a thousand starlit nights

I have felt the breath of your kiss as the wind played along my neck

I have felt the touch of your fingers in the moonlight streaming down from the heavens

I have seen deep into your soul, a soul as deep as the cosmos

And yet, we have never met

Nor do we even know of each other

The very essence of our beings tells us that the other is there

Yet we are unaware of what our lives could be

Someday, possibly, we will unite

Together we will wreak havoc through the universe

Fueled by love eternal, there is no-one who can stop us from sharing a radical love with the world

A love that says we will not be beaten

We will not be hindered

And we will not give up

A love that will see us through death itself, and into the waiting arms of infinity

Which may itself not be able to contain us

Out of the hallowed halls of the Dreamlands I awake from slumber.

A longing for one I have not felt in æons past permeates my soul.

I can still feel the touch of her hair as she reclines against me.

The air hangs heavy with her scent.

My arms close around the bare skin of her waist, and for a moment, she is still here.

One brief moment between the waking world, and that otherworld of what could be,

Of what could have been,

And sometimes what might yet come.

One brief moment I feel her presence as the touch of our astral forms unite us as one.

Then it is gone.

Away, into the æther it floats, leaving nothing but the remembrance and longing of a moment.

A moment never to be repeated.

What do you say when the words refuse to come

When you reach into the aether and grasp at thoughts that become incorporeal at your touch

How do you draw these into the natural world, and breathe life into them

It is fear

They can feel it, smell it, taste it

They know when you are afraid to leave your comfort zone, and so they elude you

They wait for you to acknowledge and face your fears

For you to become worthy to transcribe them to paper

There are many things that I desire to say, yet fear keeps me from them

It wounds me, not as with a sword, but a thousand, thousand flays from a razor

The words mock me, and my insecurities, hurling jabs and whittling down my resolve

I will conquer them someday

Today may not be that day, but soon

I will overcome my fears, and I will reach into the aether and lay claim to the words that I long to say

The words my heart needs to speak

For good or ill, I will leave my comfort zone

And no matter the outcome, I will be better for it

For I will be afraid no longer

I will let my heart speak

I cannot be your lover

I can love you without end

Unceasing

Unfailing

But I cannot be your lover

I can hold you through your darkest nights

Cry with you

Reassure you

Show you how very much I love you

But I cannot be your lover

The moon and stars dance locked an embrace

One they have danced since Creation

So too would I hold you throughout eternity

But your arms will eventually tire

Because I cannot be your lover

Those very same lights I would snatch from the sky

If only I did not already see them in your eyes

You cannot give to someone what they already possess

Were the world at my command, I would grant it to you as well

Your plaything, to do with as you like

I would give you anything your heart desired

To the ends of the earth and beyond

In order to show my love for you

But for as much as I love you

Cherish and adore you

I cannot be your lover

A time will come when you hurt no more

Pain is gone and feelings fade

You will move on, and rightly so

I would stay by your side until that day

Always caring

Always loving

Always radiating your worth back to you

To show you that you are loved

You are cared for

You are tended

You are safe

Until that day comes that I am no longer needed

But for as long as you need these things

These reminders

This promise

That I can't not be your lover

*Hope, Betrayal, Redemption*

Hands

Warm hands

Soft hands

Strong hands

His hands

Hands that I have never felt before

Hands that pick me up when I am down

Safe hands

Hands I did not know I needed until they grasped mine

Why his hands

Why him

Indeed, why even a "he"

Never before in my life have I been taken by a man

Never before have I become drunk on the sight, the smell, the touch of a boy

But then along comes him

A knight in shining armor

Coming to save the Princess who seeks to lose herself

Another thing I have never desired

Always before, when I have given my heart to one, I was the protector

The comforter

The lover

Bestowing affection and companionship on whatever fancy had caught my heart's eye

Never did I seek recompense

Only to hold one and let them know that they were loved

And yet

Everything that I desired to give to these precious girls that have graced the walls of
my heart and the touch of my pen

These things I crave from him

Many of my friends have loved me and guided me

Made me feel like a real girl

But he makes me feel like a woman

One who trusts enough to be vulnerable before him

Because she knows that she is safe

His hands

Those hands

How I long to see what is at the other end of those

The arms that could hold me in the darkest nights of the soul

The shoulders broad enough to carry my pains and fears

And maybe, just maybe, possibly

In the farthest flung hopes and wildest dreams

A tight embrace

A kiss on the head

And a whisper

Short and sweet

"You are enough"

Smitten.

The word comes to me again, as it has so many times this past moon.

This time, however, it comes to me  in power.

The power of word and phrase, which the Universe has given me the ability to bend.

It permeates my mind, nay, my entire being, and compels me to pull the thoughts from the aether

To give them corporeal form.

Smitten.

To be deeply affected, struck strong by feelings of attraction, infatuation, affection.

I have experienced these many times before, but this time, like so many other things in my life now, is different.

The possibility was there, I knew.

He was cute.

Caring.

Safe.

It's funny how my entire life has been about safety, yet over the course of the last ten months, it has changed in scope.

Always before, I sought to provide those I care for with safety.

To shelter them from the storms of life.

To be a rock for them to anchor themselves to.

A safety net for when they fell.

And now, as I am no longer timidly approaching my destiny, but boldly facing it tooth and claw, I have become the one who seeks those things.

A warrior, yes, for I have fought long and hard,

But a warrior princess, because I have won my crown.

Smitten.

"You look like a Princess."

Those words have echoed in my ears for near a week now,

And it was with those words that he captured my heart and soul.

Daily, the fear threatens to consume me.

What if it's a joke?

What if I'm seeing things that are not true.

Watching and waiting to see how I will ruin this one, as I always do.

Then I see his face, his eyes, his safe arms, and all fears and worries are banished.

That those arms would hold me at night, when loneliness and panic set in.

The fear of everything that may not or must not be.

All those are forgotten, washed away by the security that those arms hint at.

The peace promised by the thought of his fingers running through my hair as I rest upon his shoulder.

The total vulnerability of falling asleep with my head against his chest,

The beating of his heart like a war cry, chasing away my demons

Hurt as I have been before, I will not run from this one, but I will stand firm against my demons.

Steadfast in the hope that he may finally be the one.

Because until the day that he leaves my side I will remain,

Unashamedly and unabashedly,

Smitten.

How do you atone for the sins which you have committed

Not against the laws of any god or man

No, those sins which have been laid on something far more precious

The heart of your fellow man

Led as sacrificial lambs to one who knows nothing of love

Only pain

Healer, I called myself

Drawn to the broken and innocent

How many times has my trusted hand led them to  pain

How many times more must it happen before I have learned

A healer, I am not, but a harbinger of woe

A siren singing a call of longing

A mad woman leaving destruction in her wake

Old and lonely, afraid to love

More terrified to be loved

Walking an empty road, the ones she hurt laid out behind her

Nothing but poetry to mark the places where they fell

Where she abandoned them

Empty words bearing empty promises

Rewritten to fit her narrative

She had done what was right

What was true

What was necessary

When will she learn, when will she say "Enough"

When we she find one for which she says "No. I will not harm this one."

When will she atone

When will she stop running from what she has wrought

From the pain she has caused

When will she face her demons

The monsters that small children fear lie under their beds

I do not fear the monster under the bed, for we are well acquainted

I am the monster under the bed

Knight in shining armor,

Did you come to save me from myself?

Did you think you could slay the beast that lies inside?

Did you give even a moment's pause as you stepped over the bones of those who thought the same?

Or did you think that you were better than them?

That you were more gallant than them?

That you were special?

Untouchable.

But your kind never learn, do they?

Each of you as foolish as the last.

Moreso, actually.

You see the wounds, hear the tales, and yet still try to come and claim your prize.

That is all my tower is to you.

A game.

A monster to be defeated.

A princess to be saved.

Golden lands to sail off to until we reach the end of our days.

You should not have been shocked to find out your princess was the monster.

You could not kill one and keep the other.

Foolish gallant "knight".

Your banners are woven of burlap.

Your weapons are a stick and cauldron lid

Your horse, some cloth and stuffing mounted on a pole.

You were never a knight, my dearest,

You were just a fuckboy.

But then I was never a princess either.

I was just your fucktoy.

"Can we to back to how it was before", you ask.

How far back do you want to go?

Can we even go back to how it was then?

Shall we go back to the pinnacle?

When my heart was yours and my body was at your command.

When I gave you parts of me yet untouched.

Not that you bothered to reach out and take it.

Back before you said you wished you could love me.

Do we go back farther, to when you were my protector?

Where you said you would always protect me and I told you it would just hurt you.

Where you said I would never hurt you.

Where you said you would never let someone hurt me.

Well look at us now, both licking our wounds.

At least I can admit it.

Back to the very beginning, when we were just passing acquaintances?

Two people who met by chance from a common location.

A simple "Hi" and smile to suffice for conversation.

Truth is, it does not matter how far back we go.

Even if we travelled to the dawn of time, I would still have a hole where you unraveled my heart.

And so I walk away, holding on to what is left of my soul while you hold the yarn in your hands.

And I walk.

And I walk.

Hole growing ever larger.

But you won't let go.

Did you block my number when you removed me as a friend?

I'm not sure which is worse, that you did, or that you kept all the people I introduced to you

Did you even feel it when you removed me from your life?

If you're just pretending to put a wall between us, you're doing an awful good job of it.

There wasn't a day I saw you that you didn't play with my hair.

Rest your chin on my head.

Hug me with everything in you.

And now you ignore me.

Avoid me.

Look at me with hate and contempt in your eyes.

Honestly, getting over you would be easier without that last one.

Mostly though, you have the nerve to act as if I am to blame.

After I gave you my life and you crumpled it.

Tossed it aside.

Destroyed it with words that cannot be unsaid.

Your lips said that you wanted to go back to how we were before,

But your actions speak a thousand words more.

We can never go back.

Not with a thousand apologies.

Not with ten thousand acts of love.

Fool me once, shame on you.

Fool me twice… shame on me.

Not that I have anything left to fool me with.

Not after you shattered my heart and ripped my soul from me.

No, we can never go back, my love.

And you are wholly to blame.

I thought I was done writing about you.

Well… I guess I'm not.

Fuck you.

Fuck every time you ever traced your fingers down my spine.

Fuck the hugs you gave me, no matter who was watching.

Fuck your fear.

You're afraid to love someone like me?

It certainly didn't seem that way.

You should try living my life if you want to know fear...

Done writing about you?

How many have I written in the last two weeks alone?

I no longer even give them the courtesy of a name.

My folder is becoming overrun with documents called "Untitled".

When did you know you were afraid?

How long did you pretend?

It doesn't matter…

You got what you wanted.

And I got the ending that I told you was inevitable.

Done writing?

Hah.

I am not even finished writing.

I wrote with hope.

I wrote with depression.

Now I write with anger.

No, I do not expect that I will be done writing anytime soon.

I still have two more stages to forgetting you.

Forgetting your breath on my neck.

Forgetting the warmth of your body against mine.

Forgetting every time you said that you would protect me.

Never hurt me.

But you did.

All because you were afraid…

Time for you to deal with what you wrought.

Grow up…

And grow some balls.

The scent of you around me

The warmth of your lips pressed 'gainst my forehead

So completely numbed me, body and soul

That I did not feel it when you stole the light, my life, from me as you withdrew


~ your only kiss

Grief, they say, is the process by which you heal

Wounds left when a dear one has left your life

It is not a strict progression, but different stages that may be played out in any order

Some skipped, some returned to

Grief, at its end, is when you accept what is gone

The memories of the other stages growing less painful over time

Anger, bargaining, denial…

I have been through these

I want to know the release of acceptance

It continues to elude me

When a loved one has departed, and you are no longer able to see them, that pain and grief is great

Imagine how much stronger it must be to grieve the loss of someone that you must continue to see

Someone who does not see you

Whose eyes glaze over when you cross their vision

That is true grief…

Forgetting someone who has already forgotten you

But yet remains always in your heart


- An echo of what once was

The couch on which we sat stands in the corner, heavy with moving boxes.

The bed on which we lay stacked in the corner, waiting to be reassembled.

A fleeting mirage passes my vision,

Where I was held so tightly in your arms that I could feel your heartbeat.

At least now I can find some small solace in the fact,

That I sleep now within walls your eyes have never seen.


~ home is where the heart heals

I remember the way walked

How you shuffled your feet

A slow steady pace

As if you were cross-country skiing

A sound that brought be so much peace

Yes, I can still hear you as you come up behind

Breath held in hope and anticipation

Right up until the moment that you turn and walk away


~ A thousand miles in a single step

Friends.

That is all, you say.

Then you consume me with your touch.

Imprison me with your hugs.

Bewitch me with the heat of your body pressed against mine.

The feeling of your breath on my neck.

Your scent on my clothes.

But we are just friends.

Why then do your lips say one thing, when every other part of you screams something else?

Which am I to believe?

At one point, I belonged to you.

Your toy to play with as you chose.

But no longer.

I have my own will, and a broken heart to heal.

A mind to return to peace.

And so I wake up and dress in my cutest clothing,

Strap an unlocked collar 'round my neck.

To show you,

To remind myself,

That I belong to me.

That I am,

Unowned.

I know I said I would not write of you again

Digital words barely dry on the figurative page

I knew then that they were a lie

As did everyone who read them

So many things said between us, both spoken and unspoken

Maybe I was a little hasty though

Slowly, we will rebuild

Back to the friendship that we enjoyed before

I wish now that I could take back some of the things I have written in anger

In despair

In desperation

And in hate

Things I should have never said for emotions I wasn't sure I felt

Because at the end of all things, standing there in the bitter cold

Your body wrapped around me, warming mine with your embrace

Shielding me from the wind

I realised I was in the place where I belonged

Were you a fool, yes

But I a fool much bigger

Three undeniable truths I know…

In your eyes there is fire

Energizing me

Inspiring me

Threatening to burn anything that may oppose me

In your voice, there is cool running water

It soothes me

Washes away my fears

And floods over my demons, sending them past the ninth gate

In your arms, there is safety

A net to catch me when I fall

Strength to support me when mine has failed

And a warmth that fills my heart

These are three truths I know about you

And I will not let them go of them again

Will I ever stop the quickening of my heart when you hold me close?

I should hope not.

Will I ever not feel an electric surge when you call me honey?

It is sweeter to my ears than its namesake is to the tongue.

Will there ever come a day that just having you by my side brings comfort and peace?

That day would be truly dark indeed.

Because you, my darling, are a bright ray of light in the darkness.

A beacon that shines, guiding me back to myself.

My protector.

And my comforter.

I have heard others say that love is hell.

If this be true,

If this be love,

Then I have no desire to see Heaven.

It's funny sometimes

How you

Keep on waiting

For the shoe to drop

Anxiously awaiting when your

Whole world crumbles

But instead of another shattering

Another heartbreak

Another spiral of self-loathing and despair

The one who holds the shoe

Upon which you stare with bated breath

Instead places it upon your feet

Lifts you up

And says

"Would you like to

Come dance with me?"

It is so very funny

When you, a writer

Who sits there carefully crafting line after line

Drawing out every exquisite drop of emotion from each letter penned

Can with just the simplest of words

A small phrase or two

Be rendered completely speechless

Left blushing

By things so innocently spoken

Through the lips of your lover

I wrote before of your poisoned kiss

Lips dripping sweetly with sedative

And how you removed the life within me as you drew away

Yet most thing are not as they appear

And others must happen before dreams may unfurl

So I drank greedily from the pain of that twisted kiss

Twisted, though, is not the word

Unripe

Not quite yet ready

Premature

I say this now because when those lips touch mine

When your scent is around me once more

And the warmth of your body knocks away the chill

That breath which once brought death

Now sparks joy in me

Ignites hope

Rekindles love

And banishes the darkness

As you breathe life most precious once more into my soul

I saw you today

The first time in eternity

And our eyes locked for a brief moment

Short enough to barely be a greeting between strangers

Long enough for all the forgiveness I thought I gave you

Bubble up like poison through my veins

But this time, He was there

Standing beside me, holding me

His arms drawing out the venom that you left

In a wound that would not heal

I am not your average girl

No stitch of hair upon my head

Five-o-clock shadow on my face

A deep, raspy voice that I try to hide from him

But still he stays

Depression is my oldest friend

Fear, anxiety, and self-loathing there as well

A host of mental issues, both real and imaginary

But still he stays

He has walked with my through my highest peaks

Only to turn round and see me submerged in mire

And picked me up and carried me to stable ground

Because he stays

When my demons come to taunt me

And the whole world seems to turn away

When I have lost my hope, my light

He comes to me

Cradles me in his arms

Places a kiss upon my head

Tells me that he loves me

And that through all of this

He will stay

*Those Who Walked Beside Me*

The poems in the section are dedicated to my closest friends, those that have stood beside me throughout my darkest times, and also shared my joys with me.  It has been an honor to know each of you.  I would not be here without the love and support that you have shown me throughout the years.

Blue Butterfly sat upon Sunflower and sighed,

"Oh how I long to be like you.

From smallest seed you have grown,

To towering over your kin.

Fighting against the gravity of the world.

Yet you remain bold and beautiful,

Your face shining back towards the sun,

In defiance of everything against you."

Sunflower smiled at Blue Butterfly.

"Oh my precious friend, but don't you see,

I too desire to be as you.

For I was just a seed, and I grew and grew.

But you,

You grew, and you died to yourself.

A process long and arduous.

And when finished, rose from the cocoon of your old self,

Shiny, new, and magnificent"

She continued,

"You see, we all have our different battles,

And each of us must fight them our own way.

But what matters in the end, is not how you got through it,

But that you got through it.

And who you got through it with."

Blue Butterfly thought on this a moment.

"These words are true, my friend.

Battles both lost and won,

Each day closer to victory.

It is indeed those who stand beside us who make us strong.

I am proud to fly here by your side,

And glad that you sit so firmly at mine."


~ For Casey, my sunflower queen

"I am having a bad day" I say

The words come more often than I would like

"It's okay," she says. "We will deal with it."

It's always 'we' with her

She will not let me fight alone

Kicking and screaming, she will drag me back to my happiness

As she has done for so long now

To be honest, I have given up fighting her on it

A simple 'okay' as I acquiesce to her aid

A sword and shield

High Lady of my Queensguard

Before, I had a Sword and a Shield

However, they we wielded by separate warriors

She takes up both, refusing to let me fall

She brings peace when I am broken

Resolve when I require a push

And a Light when I have lost my way

What I have done in this life, or any past to deserve her

I only thank the Universe that I am allowed to call her 'friend'


~ For Carman, my gentle guiding hand

Who am I that you would call me friend?

What have I done to deserve one like you?

Though we have but barely met, I look up to you so much.

You are the younger me that I was not allowed to be.

I see in you so much of who I long to be.

So much of who I have strained and yearned to be.

Hold on to your youth, while you still have it.

Cherish it, and revel in it while it is still yours,

Lest you grow to be old like me.

Jaded and bitter, holding on to every scrap of the life you did not live.

It is beginning again

One whom I cherish more than life itself, though she is not able to be mine

I have always said that each one was different, that each one was special

This has never been truer in her case

In less than the course of a month, she has become a closest friend

Indeed, she has obliterated my shields, and seen the parts of me that I hide

Less than thirty days, and she has seen into the darkness of my soul

Already, she has proved herself as a comforter and a friend

She makes me desire to do better by myself

Moreso than most have

She makes me want to be a better person

Someone who would be worthy of her, were she not already taken

She has made me look deeper into myself

Encouraged me to find the things that were wrong and fix them

She encourages me to be me

Not for others, but for myself

To be able to be the best me that I can be, for the sake of myself and my happiness

She reflects me, in all my imperfections,

So that I can see what must be changed to be who I truly am

Who she already sees and accepts me for

It is rare for anyone to mean this much to me in such a short moment of time

For her, it took only and introduction, and I was spellbound

A great friendship will bloom from this, I know

I only pray I do not let her down.

Lo, see now as she comes

The maiden of fire

Forged in the flames of her element

She has come to take her place at my side

Long have I wondered

As the embodiment of water, those who bear the kiss of flame are tricky

Yet through it all, she has proven loyal to me

Ready to take up arms and secure her place in my closest circle

It has not been without doubt

Indeed, my darkest nights of the soul have been due to her

Yet she has proven her dedication to me, to my fight

I take pride in awarding her the place of honor as the Guardian of Fire in my most
loyal retinue

Surely it is to be said that they seek after those who challenge them the most

As the guardian of Water, her flames threaten to consume me

Bit I will not be swayed

I will stand firm

And I will love her with all that is in me

For through her fire, Steam may once again be processed,  that element which has
triggered progress for far so long

And in it, I may yet feel a bit of warmth

As it stands, she remains my Queensguard of Fire

And I will fight all in her honor

Until I am dead, or there are no battles left to be fought

For she remains so,

I would live for her

Until the Earth burns, and the seas boil

I will stay vigilant

I will not run

I will uphold the faith she puts in me

Because she means the world to me

And I dare not disappoint


~ For Heidi, my steadfast warrior

What did I do to deserve you?

How is it I came to call you friend?

You stand by me when I could not bear to look at myself.

You hold me by the hand when I walk upon the edge of a precipice

When there is nothing but darkness all around, you come bearing a torch.

When all has turned to nothing and my strength has failed, you whisper words to keep me moving.

To keep me fighting.

To keep me strong.

Together, we can do things that I alone could not imagine.

With you, I am unbreakable.

Alongside you, I will go strong.

I will be the person that you believe I am.

It is the very least that I can do for you.

For you have faith in me when I do not.

And for that, I am forever grateful.

Four souls have come together to vie for control of my pen and the gift that it bears

Like four stalwart sentinels on the battlefield, they stand, sizing each other up

It is a game of chess that they play, a testing of mettles

Every so often, one will step forward in a show of power and strength

Four there are, standing in opposition, yet it is merely a sparring exercise

For most

One who is there was once as the others

My Queensguard

Yet her light has faded and she has veered from the spot she once held

Still the other three stand

Guiding me, guarding me

They are the shoulders that I lean on when I am too weak to stand on my own

They are the ones who share my deepest secrets

My darkest fears

They stand with shields held against my insecurities and weaknesses, and guide me
back to my Light

My Ladies of Light

I thank you from the bottom of my heart

You are each more special to me than you know

*The Early Years*

Love,

A strange and fickle plant.

If left untended, it grows rampant, turning to lust.

An all-consuming need that destroys everything.

If cared for only partially, it will return only empty love.

Love that is one-sided.

One where there are no participants, only actors.

Yet, if tended properly and well nourished,

If frequently weeded to remove the things that try to spring up in its place,

It grows into a miraculous fruit.

Tender, sweet, pleasing to the eye.

One gets basically what one puts into it.

Often, it has a hard, protective skin around it.

If you can work gently enough to breach this,

You will be amazed at what you can find.

And if you continue to nurture it, even after this,

You will see it blossom into a tree that will support you all your life.

Take care that you not bruise it though.

Or it will return to a vine that will encompass and choke you.

Because love is a strange and fickle plant.

Love.

What is its true purpose?

Sometimes, I truly believe that it exists only for pain.

It seems that we always love the ones we don't want to.

When we do find the one we want, we don't take the chance.

Too many people mistake sex for love.

Sex is only for pleasure; you can buy it for gods' sakes.

Love on the other hand is for complete euphoria.

Sometimes, I don't even want a relationship.

Right now, for example.

I don't want a girlfriend right now.

I just want someone to hold me.

I want to spend hours just holding and kissing.

Not tongue-jabbed-down-throat kissing either.

Real kissing, the soft kind that sends shivers down your spine.

The kind that makes your eyes roll back in your head.

The kind you wish would never end.

I want to sit in your lap and lean back against you.

Want to feel the soothing warmth of your body.

I want to wake up, still in your arms.

Even if it is just that one time.

Love?

I guess it's the real drug.

For the short time we experience it, it take the pain away.

Makes us forget we had been hurt.

Hell, makes us forget everything except how we feel at the moment.

Like all drugs though, it only lasts for that one moment.

A temporary relief to a terminal pain.

The comedown's a mother too.

After the initial feeling is gone, you look for it everywhere.

Sometimes even in places you loathe.

Then, after time, the pain dulls.

Well, you get used to it actually; it's still just as strong.

You don't actively look for it as much anymore.

Gods forbid anyone mention it though.

You'll be right back out there, following even the smallest scent.

Then, you'll wake up one morning, sigh, and realize that you don't need it anymore.

Feels good to be free again, doesn't it?

To not be dependent.

To not be constantly searching.

That's when it hits you in the ass again.

Bang, zoom, and you're right back where you started.

Probably don't even remember anything about the night it happened either, do you?

I told you, love is one hell of a mother.

By the gods, it's worth it though.

Even if it is just for that one night.

Me?

How do I know?

Heh,

Cause I'm the poster-child for addiction to it.

Addicted to the look of it,

Addicted to its smell,

Addicted to the sound,

Addicted to you, and the thought of spending a night wrapped up in your arms.

Be my drug for one night?

Help me forget my pain?

Let me live one more short, eternal moment?

I won't tell a soul, I promise.

Our secret.

Hell, everyone has their little fixes.

Chocolate for some, soda for others.

For me, it's love.

And you.

Living and surviving.

I am alive, yet am I truly living?

Or rather, am I just surviving?

Just barely getting by.

I have nothing to live for, no one to love, no one to love me.

It did not hurt at much at first,

But then to have love, and have it ripped away,

I would have rather been killed.

Now all I do is sit from day to day,

Wondering if I should even continue on to the next.

There is nothing for me.

I work, then I sleep.

There is no such thing as fun, pleasure, enjoyment.

These words are foreign to me.

Despair, loneliness, depression,

These are the words of my vocabulary, and most times, my only friends.

If I could find but one to love me,

'Twould give me reason enough to live,

But until then, I must go on like this.

Surviving.

Princess Couplets: An Ongoing Story of Hope.

Date Unknown (c. 2002-2003?):

One by one the petals fall until the princess is revealed

But how many flowers must wilt and die before she knows her name.

Date Unknown (c. 2005-2006?):

Day by day did she slumber deep, her identity unknown

But now no more flowers shall wither away, for she has come to claim her throne.

08/14/11

Days turned to months, and months to years, as Princess did lay siege

To finally grasp within her hands the dreams she once believed.

07/16/12

Little Princess, she did dance, as the rain cleansed all her fears.

Now fully awoken, she will dance once more, the Dance kept secret through the years

03/14/13

Forgotten princess all alone, lay naked and neglected

Yet through new friends, light shines again, as she now knows she is respected.

10/31/14

Tortured princess cried out in pain, those friends both near and far

Came to help her stand again, and wash away the scars

12/31/15

Warrior princess, standing firm, sword drawn, and balance steady

All her demons and her foes are wary, for they know she is now ready

12/31/16

Darling princess, see her walk unscathed, though the flames burn all around

She has fought her demons, won her war, and stands now ready to be crowned

12/25/17

Newborn Queen upon the ramparts, gazing near and far

Taking stock of all her lands that for which she fought so very hard

12/25/17

Fledgling Queen, she comes now to court, her Queensguard at her side

To call to task all of her foes who would see her crown denied

A painted smile,

A frown that's carved.

Wooden faces line the boulevard.

Joy, despair, grief, and relief,

I am the Maker of the Mask.


You see me laugh and hide a grin,

Turn round, turn back, a slump I'm in.

Blink once or twice and you could miss,

A profound look with thoughts adrift.

I am the Wearer of the Mask.


Pry off the mask only to find,

A man-made façade of a different design.

Man or woman, boy or girl?

Dare you look deeper to unfurl,

The Soul under the Mask

I'm sorry.

To try and push away the only one I care about.

Is that not truly dumb?

Since we met, have you not always been there for me.

Always helped me,

Always listened to me.

How could I put you through so much?

I deliberately tried to push you away.

Why?

For some imagined reason.

To think that I would lose my only friend over something imagined.

Is that not truly pathetic?

I only hope that you can forgive this lonely fool.

Words...

Both the substance and the methods of my gift.

For nearly two decades now have I crafted with the written word.

Things left unsaid, words to never be heard in the light of day.

Like a burst of raw emotion, they now come floating to my mind...

Only to flit to into the aether before they can be brought to meaning.

Dancing around, they taunt and tease at me.

Perhaps it is because I have left them to be dormant for so long.

For a long time now have I occupied my mind with things to dull it, instead of sharpening.

Nay, that is but a half-truth, and a poor one at that.

Truly it must be said that I have preoccupied my demons with baubles to keep them at bay.

Now, with nothing but the open road before me, they have finally come to call.

In a way, it must be said to be a good thing, for here I sit scratching out these words.

Words first given birth in the heart...

Given form in the mind...

Finally to be given voice through this pen.

I can now begin to feel the chains that have bound my gift for so long begin to come undone.

The words that have seemed to breathed their own life pattern themselves unaided.

They call to me to look deeper within myself and beckon me to draw them into existence.

Sleeping, though, they seem to be, not yet ready to be awakened.

Let us now bide our time and allow them to mature.

When their time comes, they will dawn upon the world in their radiant glory and unmatched splendour.

And I will stand by them, the longings of my heart, singing of their beauty for all the world to hear.

I am here,

Alone,

Wanting you.

You are there,

Far away,

Away from me.

I ran you away by not showing that I cared for you,

By not being there for you.

By not saying that I loved you.

I am sorry that I caused the pain,

That now runs through you,

So please,

Find somebody new.


~ *The first words I wrote*